PEACE!

BE

STILL!

Exodus 14:14 (New King James Version)
"The LORD will fight for you, and you shall hold your peace."

The Unfinished Story of My Life

BY

MARIE NADEIGE MAURICE

A STORY THAT WILL CHANGE THE READER'S LIVES FOREVER!

Xulon PRESS

CONTENTS:

PROLOGUE:

I decided to write this book because the Lord placed it heavily on my heart one Friday morning at about ten o'clock on September 9, 2005. I was trying to figure out what I was going through at that particular time in my life. The Holy Spirit of God touched my life at that moment to write these things down – not just about that season I was currently facing in my life, but about every single thing that I had experienced. I did not hesitate, for I knew if I followed the instructions of the Holy Spirit, my life would never be the same again. I knew I would be set free from emotional bondages and the readers would also be made whole. This decision was not my number one choice in life. Nevertheless, I know that my prayer to God has always been "use me Lord, I will do whatever You want me to do; I will go wherever You send me, and I will say whatever You want me to say." Therefore, I determined to write this book because the Lord commanded me to do so. The devil would not have put this great idea into my heart because all he is here to do is to destroy what God builds, if God allows him. I definitely know this assignment is God's calling for me because I think any person whose life story is as complicated, challenging, and confusing as mine would not voluntarily begin to talk or write about it without either being pushed by some type of supernatural power or knowing that s/he would find a solution from the readers. I am simply following God's instructions by faith. Everyone who reads or hears about this book will benefit from it.

As you read my life story, you will learn about my background, my personal relationship with God, my good and bad experiences, and my saddest and happiest times in life. I will try my best to remember as much as I can. There are many things that happened in my life in which I do not recall the exact date, time, and year, but I do remember the episode as fresh as if it were yesterday. I also would like my readers to be aware that everything said in this story is true. In addition, this story is intentionally written to bless and transform readers of all ages, for no one is exempt from the things I have experienced. Therefore, as long as the readers know how to read and understand what they read, this narrative is meant for you. No matter who you are, where you are from, where you have been, what you are going through or what your circumstances are, I pray you will find something with which you can relate. This book will tell you whatever happened or will happen in your life is for a specific reason. Sometimes the circumstances people go through are not explained to them, but God knows it all and will always remain faithful according to His will. He will eventually show you the way.

Writing this book is the most wonderful thing that had ever happened to me, besides experiencing the presence of the Lord. Anybody who has an intimate relationship with God knows there is nothing that can compare with being in His glorious presence. I also realized what has happened is happening and will happen to me; I have something to share with other people for the glory of God. No matter what is going on in your life, God can use that particular circumstance to save someone else. In fact, it is a blessing to recognize a life without problems is life without lessons. Therefore, everything that seems to make life difficult is considered an opportunity for spiritual growth.

One other reason why this story is being written is to glorify the name of the Lord for even thinking about creating me and placing me on this planet and most importantly, saving me for eternity. If I really decided to write about what the Lord Almighty has done for me, and what He has brought me through, one book would not have been enough because I have so much to say.

In my opinion, this manuscript is intended to be humorous. I hope it will make you laugh, cry, get angry, be sad and/or happy.

This book will be written mostly in English, but you will also find some Haitian Creole, French, and even some Spanish quotes. Translations are provided. However, I pray that the Holy Spirit will reveal the true meaning to you according to your needs.

In this volume, I am going to try my best, by the grace of God, to summarize my life story as much as I can, and if it is God's will for me to continue to share my story through writing, I will do so. My prayer to God is that this book will truly make a difference in the lives of the readers.

Opening words of Praise

Lift up your hands and begin to worship the Lord regardless of your circumstances. Thank Him for what is going on in your life right now. Glorify His Holy Name. He deserves all the glory! The harder is pain, the sweeter the victory. He is Jehovah Shalom, the Prince of Peace. He is the beginning and the end, the first and the last. No one came before Him, nor did anyone come after Him. I dare you to praise His Name right where you are no matter what your agony is! Lord, I thank you. I magnify your Name, for you are the Bright Morning Star. I have no other choice but to give

You praise and honor. Heavenly Father, please accept my praise offerings, and allow me to worship You for Who You are. Thank you for all you have done for me. Lord, I pray every single person who has a chance to read this book will be set free from all bondages. In Jesus' name I pray, Amen!

Bible Verses on Praise & Worship

Psalm 9:1(NKJV): "I will praise You, O LORD, with my whole heart; I will tell of all Your marvelous works."

Psalm 26:7 (NJKV): "That I may proclaim with the voice of thanksgiving, and tell of all Your wondrous works."

Psalm 75:1 (NKJV): "We give thanks to You, O God, we give thanks! For Your wondrous works declare that Your name is near."

Psalm 107:1 (KJV): "O give thanks unto the LORD, for he is good: for his mercy endures forever."

Psalm 136:1(NLT): "Give thanks to the Lord, for he is good! His faithful love endures forever."

Insights and Acknowledgments:

You might be reading this book and you do not have any of the following: family, friends, job, shelter, or money. Even if you feel like the whole world is against you or you are in an abusive relationship, please allow me to tell you that you are not alone. The Lord is on your side. The word of God says, "Come those who are weary and tired and God will give you rest" (Matthew 11:28). No matter what you are facing right now, God is the answer.

A special thanks to the following individuals who, without their contributions and support to my inspiration, knowledge, and other help, this book would not have been written:

Family: My mother, Marie L Jean-Charles thanks for being the vessel used by God to give me life.

My father Jean-Claude Etienne thanks for bringing me to the United States.

My stepfather Frantzcy Charles thanks for providing for me through my teenage years.

My former husband, Rimane Maurice thanks for being the father of my daughter.

My beautiful five-year-old daughter Hadassah M Morris thanks for loving mommy.

My sisters Natacha Etienne, Emmanuela St. Just, Stephany Charles, Sylvie Charles, Marie E. (Sandy) Charles, and Roseland Charles

My brothers Romeo Etienne, Schmid Etienne, Guerdy F. Charles,

My aunts: Marie-Luce Jean, Lunance Jean, Enide Jean

My uncle: Jean Denel Jean

All my cousins, nieces, and nephews.

Mentors: Pastor Jamane Esperans, Pastor Emma Soy, Pastor Paul Bertrand, Pastor Jean Bertrand, Pastor Charlie Jeanty and Kelly O'Malley, Sony Desir, Pastor Ruth Marseille

Organizations: Harry S. Truman College, Northeastern Illinois University, First Bank and Trust of Evanston, Easter Seals Metropolitan Chicago, Between Friends, Life Span, St. Francis Hospital, Northshore Senior Center Social Services, Xulon Press

Friends: Patricia O'Connor, Kidziah and Vince, Brenda and Adam, Yanique Lauture, Rose Azor, Yvrose Joseph, Rene Chapel, Rose Lamour, Gigi, Elizabeth, Midline and Rodney Bien-Aime, Ruth and Pharis Mondesir, Josue and Jonace Pierre

Readers: A special thanks to all my readers who consider this book to be part of your bookshelf collection. I pray as you read this you would experience tremendous peace, joy, and freedom you have never experienced before. Please allow me to encourage you to be still and cast all your care at the feet of Jesus who is your maker and has plans for you and your family.

Chapter One

MY CHILDHOOD

"I have been ordained by God while I was still in my mother's womb." (Psalm 139:16)

My name is currently Marie Nadeige Maurice, but used to be Marie Nadeige Etienne before I was married. According to my parents, I was born in Port-au-Prince, Haiti. I grew up with my grandparents, who are now deceased. They raised me in a place called Jeremie, which is one of the small villages in Haiti.

Even though I did not know my mother and my father when I was growing up, I did not worry about asking for them because as a child, I was not allowed to ask a lot of questions. Besides, I was too young to think that I needed them that much anyway. As a matter of fact, I was fed, bathed, and clothed, so nothing bothered me back then. My grandparents were wealthy; they were farmers and owned a lot of land throughout the village. As a result, they were known as the richest people there back in the early seventies. They used to raise animals such as cows, goats, pigs, and chickens. They also grew all kinds of fruits and vegetables that included but was not limited to potatoes, tomatoes, spinach, corn, oranges, grapefruits, avocados, manioc, yams, and more. My grandparents also grew a lot of cocoa and coffee beans. When the time of harvest came, they used to sell some of their fruits and vegetables, so they could have money to buy what they did not grow from their gardens, like rice, wheat, and some other crops.

I had a happy childhood. However, as I became mature in age, I realized my grandparents were not my biological parents; I understood well that they were my mother's parents. To tell you the truth, I do not remember how old I was when I asked my grandparents for my mom and dad, and they told me they were living in Port-au-Prince, which is the capital of Haiti.

Then, I accepted everything I was told – being a child, I believed and obeyed everything. All I knew was grandma was a great lady, and grandpa was a hard worker. I am privileged to say that my grandparents tried their best to create a comfortable environment and a beautiful life for me as a child. I can remember getting up in the morning going to the garden to pick up fruits and vegetables to eat. The scent of the morning dew was unforgettable; I could not ignore the beautiful sunrise, the sounds of different birds singing, and the voices of neighbors and passengers saying good morning and wishing "have a great day" to each other as they started their day. Everyone seemed extremely happy and grateful to be alive and enjoy life. There was a great deal of unity among the people who lived in the village. Everybody was kind to each other and available in the time of need. I believe that was a way for me as a child to be exposed to some form of peace through human relations.

It was routine for me to go to the rivers three times a day to get fresh fountain water for my parents and me to use in the house. There were two different rivers called Dlo Likso and Dlo Kolet that I used to go to. I would go to Dlo Likso mostly in the morning, but I would visit Dlo Kolet to do laundry and to shower during the day when the sun was hot.

It's safe to say everybody loved me because I was outgoing, smart, and well educated as a young girl. My grandparents sent me to school and taught me survival techniques. My personality and character were shaped by them even though they did not know how to read and write. They taught me how to respect others and myself. They used to tell me stories that represented diverse settings of life situations in order to prepare me for any obstacles. They also trained me how to appreciate life no matter what may come my way.

Through all the instructions I received from my grandparents, I learned not to be too attached to anything in life, for everything is temporary. In other words, when people get emotionally involved with anything or anybody, they will get their hearts broken when that thing or person is no longer accessible.

Everything in life has a beginning and an ending. **Everybody you come in contact with in life is temporary, including your parents and family members.** Just remember that nothing is permanent in this life. When you meet someone, sooner or later the relationship will come to an end. If you are married and have kids, you know those kids will grow up and leave you some day. Either you or your husband will go meet the Lord before the other. Come on now; you know when you met your best friend, s/he did not last long. That is just the way things are; there is absolutely nothing you can do about it. The only thing that lasts forever is the Word of God (Isaiah 40:8).

As a baby up to age twelve, the only closest people I ever knew were my grandparents. Unfortunately, the time had come that I had to leave my grandparents to go live with my mother. The sad part was I was not mature enough to understand how to properly thank them for all they had done for me.

In reality, I never regretted my childhood, but I feel bad for not being able to personally thank my grandparents for the positive impact they had made in my life before they passed away. Nevertheless, I am convinced God will reward them for what they did for me. It is imperative whenever you have a chance to make an impact in a child's life, never hesitate to do so because this child will remember your good endeavor for the rest of his/her life.

Even though I did not have my mother and my father there with me when I was growing up, God's peace was always there to guard my heart and protect me every step of the way. God was there with Moses when he was placed in the basket that was floating on top of the river (Exodus 2:1-10). He was also with Joseph when his own brothers sold him into slavery (Genesis 37:28). God was definitely with Isaac when Abraham, his father, put him on the altar to be sacrificed (Genesis 22:9). Consequently, as a child I did not know what my future held, but God had a plan for my life without me even knowing (Jeremiah 29:11). I did not comprehend what having a relationship with the Lord was at that time of my life, but I strongly believe He carried me through with His peace that passes all understanding. I would like to take this opportunity to encourage you to know the Lord will never leave you nor forsake you, no matter what you are going through (Hebrews 13:5). Because He is your Creator, He will always create a way for you.

Chapter Two

MY TEENAGE YEARS

"My life is not a mistake, but instead a miracle!"

Psalm 139:13

When I was eleven going on twelve years of age, my grandparents started getting too old to care for me. In other words, they seemed to run out of energy to provide for the family. Consequently, one of my aunts decided to take me back to Port-au-Prince because she thought as I was becoming a teenager, I needed to be with my mother. When she came to get me from Jeremie, I was excited about moving to a new place, but I didn't know what was waiting for me and how miserable my life was going to be. On the other hand, it was also sad for me to leave my grandparents I had known for so many years.

By the time I was a teenager, I was living with my mother. Now I want my readers to visualize this. When I met my mom, she was not with my father. She was not married yet, but she was living with another man with whom she had children. Therefore, I experienced two types of transitions in my life at that time. One, I was a girl who was changing into a woman, which I considered to be one of the most confusing and challenging stages in my life. I was never around people who talked about puberty. I had no idea what to expect and how to cope with it. It seemed to me that I was in a stage of confusion in my life in which I did not know how to behave and had no one to talk to about what I was going through. Transforming from a child to a teenager was one of the most difficult phases in my life.

Second, I was dealing with a stepfather and stepsiblings. In addition to that, my mother and I had never had a relationship; we never bonded since birth. Based on the information I collected from my mother, I was taken away from her when I was born. Then, she got me back when I was about one and a half years old. Due to the fact that she was unable to care for me and work at the same time, she took me to my grandparents at age two. Consequently, not only did I just meet my mother, but also I had already had a foundation, which was created by God through my grandparents.

I also came to realize life in the village was extremely different from life in the city. For instance, food and drink were provided to us in the village where I never felt hungry; in the city, everything had to be purchased if/when there was money. I had to learn how to adapt to that new lifestyle as quickly as I could in order to survive to the best of my ability.

I just wished that my mother or anybody else could understand the frustration that big shift created in me at that stage of my life. I could not understand it nor could I explain it. There were times I wished I could escape and go back to the village where I grew up, but I could not. Regrettably, I could not blame my mother for what I experienced at that time because it was not her fault she did not raise me, nor was it fair for her that she got pregnant with me out of wedlock. However, as a child, I had to suffer the consequences of not being born into a so-called "normal family" in which my parents were married before they had me, and most importantly both of them worked to provide for me as they raised me.

As a result, I believed my mom and I had nothing to do with this situation because God is in control of everybody's life journey from beginning to end. Nobody has control over how s/he was brought up in this life. We can only be grateful we are born human beings – at least, we seem to have more options than the some other creatures, like the animals, for example.

The first year living with my mother was not that bad because she was working and so was my stepfather. The monthly salary they both contributed did not seem enough to pay for rent and provide food for a household of about fifteen to twenty members, which included some of my aunts with children, and one uncle. Among all of those people who lived in the house, only three people were working. In addition, my sisters and my brothers were young, except for one sister who was only two years younger than me. Therefore, I used to babysit all my siblings including some of my cousins and sometimes children from the neighborhood. I had to keep them safe, bathe and feed them, wash their clothes, help them with their homework and do all the household chores.

Between the ages of thirteen and fourteen, in the late 1980's, my mom accepted Christ as her personal Savior with all of us! Of course, that was another transition in my life, but a better one. As I mentioned before, I was not allowed to ask any questions unless it was important, or it should not be anything that was happening in the house. For instance, if anything hurt me, according to the Haitian culture, I was supposed to be able to handle it, and/or act as if there is nothing going on. Besides, my family members thought I was old enough to bear whatever came my way even though I was in major pain. They also expected me to pretend or act like everything was all right in my life in front of other people.

Due to the fact that my mother became a Christian with all of us, we had to follow and adopt new concepts of life. That meant certain rules and regulations had to be examined and followed differently with a biblical point of view. I totally agreed with that new way of living because I had no choice. According to 2 Corinthians 5:17, "If someone is in Christ, s/he is a new creation; the old things have gone and the new things have come." Things were not the same anymore. Spiritually speaking, we were great, but financially speaking, my family became poorer and poorer. I mean, we were considered one of the poorest groups of people on earth. All I can remember is that my mother was working, but all of a sudden, she was not working anymore. No questions asked! My stepfather got up every morning and came back in the evenings empty-handed. It looked and sounded like he got a job, but only the Lord knew what was happening at that particular time.

Things were bad for all of us, but I am going to simply talk about my situation and how God saved me, and He still continues to bless me day after day. I used to spend days without eating. I mean no food! The reason was that my mother was not working and did not have enough money to provide for all of us. When my mother would try her best to find some food for us to eat, the little portion of food she found was not enough to be divided among so many people who lived in the house.

Taking shower or baths--forget it! I used to pass days without taking a shower. There was not enough water to drink. When I finally got some water, it was not even sufficient enough to quench my thirst. I remember being so thirsty sometimes that I could not even find words to describe that feeling. This reminds me of the Samaritan woman Jesus found at the well (John 4:1-42). I would go to someone's house to ask for some water to drink. At that time, I would take anything, even urine, as long as whatever I drank tasted, looked, or sounded like water. One thing that I know Jesus told the woman,

> "Everyone who drinks this water will be thirsty again, but whoever drinks the water I give them will never thirst. Indeed, the water I give them will become in them a spring of water welling up to eternal life."

I did not die of thirst when I was in Haiti because Jesus was my living water. Somehow, Jesus did it for me, and He can do it for you if you believe.

I also know what starving is. Starving is not something somebody explained to me or talked to me about, but it was something that became a lifestyle for me; something I experienced and something that was part of me, which is one of the reasons why I cannot see people suffer, nor do I have the heart to throw away food. I just cannot see food being wasted. I thank the Lord for giving me plenty of food to eat now.

My teenage years were not the greatest. I did not have any friends. For one reason, I was not allowed to; for another reason, I felt like I was the poorest and the most humiliated among my peers, so I figured I should not befriend anyone. I was a smart child growing up, but due to poverty that led to malnutrition, I was behind in my studies, and I even looked like I could be considered like a child with special needs. I physically looked different from my siblings in many ways. For instance, when I went out with my brothers and sisters they always looked healthier than me because I was skinny, weak, and sleepy all the time.

I remember a group of missionaries who came from the United States to help out the needy people in Haiti. Among them was a group of doctors who took x-rays of people in order to assess their health condition and determine what they needed to do to take care of them. Unfortunately, I was one of those whose x-rays revealed I was anemic. The doctors told me if I got admitted to any facility for any other health condition, I may not have the chance to recover. "dokte yo te di-m si-m kouche sou kabann mwen pap janm leve anko." *("Physicians told me if I lie on my bed I will never rise again.")* Consequently, one of the physicians gave me a prescription, but my mother could not afford to fill it. I knew that if I got sick at any given time, I might not make it; that was the scariest moment in my life.

At that time, I had something else to worry about besides food and water. I was afraid to fall asleep because I thought that I might not wake up in the morning. I had strong faith in God at that time. All I did was cry out to God for every mercy and grace. I used to attend all kinds of prayer meetings, revivals, crusades, and conferences. I knew that God's words were more powerful than the words of those doctors. For the Bible says:

Great crowds came to him, bringing the lame, the blind, the crippled, the mute and many others, and laid them at His feet; and He healed them. The people were amazed when they saw the mute speaking; the crippled made well, the lame walking and the blind seeing. And they praised the God of Israel. -Matthew 15:30-31(NIV)

Furthermore, if God was able to heal the woman with the issue of blood (Mark 5:25-34), I always had hope God could do the same for me. I realized the more trouble I encountered, the stronger my faith became. Every time the sun went down, I believed the following days would be much better than the day that had just past. My situation taught me how to live one day at a time.

I remember I used to go to sleep late and wake up early because I lived in small house that contained about fifteen people. The house had only three rooms. One of the rooms was used for the kitchen, another for the bedroom, with a full size bed in it for my mother and her husband. At night the younger kids made their beds with sheets on the floor of my mom's bedroom. The other room was used for a living room, a dining room and a guest room during the day, but turned into a bedroom at night. As a result, I had to make my bed on the floor at night to sleep. That was one of the reasons why I had to wake up so early--because the room had to be rearranged every morning before sunrise.

The harder my pains, the stronger my faith was. I believed one day, things would get better. We did not have a bathroom either, for there was not enough money to build one. I remember the house was still under construction with an unfinished bathroom and there was something on top of the roof; to my knowledge, it looked like a toilet bowl or something similar to that. During the day I used to go over people's houses to ask to allow me to utilize their bathrooms. I created a technique to go to a different house every day or whenever I needed to use it, but later the routine became so obvious that everybody in the neighborhood was aware that I did not have toilet in my house. Therefore, when I went over my neighbors' house, even for another purpose, they automatically concluded that I came either for food, which meant I was hungry, or to use their bathroom because I did not have toilet in my house.

Sometimes I felt humiliated because some people were not kind and pleasant to me due to my situation. As a matter of fact, there were times I chose to hold the stool for a long time – as long as I could because it was extremely embarrassing to me to have to go to people's house to use the toilet on a regular basis. Can you imagine holding a stool or a "poo-poo/kaka" for days? Many times, I felt sick to my stomach because some waste had to come out of my body, but I prevented it from coming out due to embarrassment.

All those dramas would occur during the day; however, when nighttime came, it was a different story. My mother provided bedpans for us so we could urinate and poop during the nights. Unfortunately, as the oldest of my siblings, I was responsible to get up early before everyone else in the neighborhood was awake to go throw the stinky stuff from the pans inside the unfinished toilet bowl on the roof of the house. That was the grossest, smelliest and the most disgusting thing to do. Sadly, I had to do it; the worst part was there were times people would see me doing it, and that was embarrassing.

I simply would like to take this time right now to give thanks to the Lord who made all these things become past tense in my life because everything I am saying has happened, but it's over; no more. Done!

There is a proverb in Creole that says, "toutotan tet poko koupe, ou espere met chapo," which means, "as long as you have your head, you hope to wear a hat." Whatever that means, it made perfect sense to me at that time – because as long as I was alive, I had the hope, someday, to have plenty of food to eat, water to drink and to shower with, clothes to wear, and a bed to sleep on. As a matter of fact, I now realize all the obstacles that I faced throughout my teenage years are now behind me. No turning back. If you are reading this book and you are going through something or anything, I mean whatever it is, just believe that the God who delivered me from my poverty, misery, and all my sufferings is able to set you free completely from whatever you are experiencing in your life today. All you need to do is trust and depend on the Lord.

"All the days of my life are destined by God" (Psalm 139:16).

Chapter Three

Nobody Said the Road Would Be Easy

**Everybody is going through something.
Whatever it may be; it can be good or bad.**

Life is a step-by-step process. In fact, as I am writing this book, my life is under construction. I am still going through some issues, but the good news is that things are not as bad as they once were. Also, I have concluded that the battle is not mine, but the Lord's. As I mentioned before, I will have to write more than one book in order to explain what I went through, what I have gone through, and what I am going through in life. It is noticeable that every time I go through something, I learn something new. I have to say writing this book is the greatest joy I have ever had in my entire life. If I had thought of this earlier, I would be able to cope with my situation much better. I am not complaining because everything happens for a reason, and nothing happens before its time. Most of the times we do not know the reason why certain things occur while we are suffering, but sooner or later we will always know why — we just have to be patient.

My life would have been more miserable if I did not have Jesus. He is the most sincere friend I have ever had. He never turns me down. He is always there and He never forsakes me. Friends come and go, but Jesus never leaves me alone, even though sometimes I feel like He is so far away. When nobody understands me, Jesus does. He is my Comforter.

Haven't you ever been in a position when you know that you know that there is war that is going on in your spirit, but you act like everything is going just great? The moment we leave church, the work place, school, or prayer conference, you wish you did not have to face the real world/life ever again. The reality is that we all are wearing a mask on a daily basis by pretending to be happy when we are sad, healthy when we are sick, wealthy when we do not even have a dime. We need to stop wearing those masks! Be real because your destiny is looking for you and cannot find you.

Another reason why we choose to lie to ourselves is because whatever we are facing is so unbelievable if anybody else is aware of exactly how we really feel, s/he will try to avoid us as much as possible. That is why we keep our circumstances to ourselves. As a matter of fact, there are times when what is going on in our lives is unexplainable. If we cannot even understand it, how can we explain it to somebody else anyway?

Sometimes I feel like in order for someone to comprehend exactly what I am going through, s/he would have to open my brain up and go to the emotional center and try to read it; then s/he would get a clear picture of what is going on in my life. Unfortunately, that is the only thing that the person would have been able to do because that particular person would not have been able to interpret the problem and find a solution for it. That is why ONLY GOD CAN DO THAT!

Every problem has a root and a foundation to begin with. Therefore, in order to get rid of any type/kind of problem/situation, we need to first find the root of it. Otherwise, the problem will keep coming back until it eats and tears us up into pieces. Only God can get into our deepest thoughts and heal our wounded hearts. No man, no relationship, no friend, no family member can satisfy like God does. He is the friend of broken hearts – the more broken a heart is, the better God can operate on it to bring it to life. The blood of Jesus is always ready to flow through all the brokenhearted, no matter how damaged they may be.

I met my father when I was seventeen years old. However, that age would be comparable to a ten-year-old child in the United States because I looked somewhat underdeveloped for my age. The only good thing I had at that time nobody could take away was my spirituality. In fact, if I did not have a spiritual foundation, I would be the most miserable person in the entire world. Spirituality became my cornerstone, my back up, and my only hope. It was (and still is) all about the level of faith I had in God that kept me alive all those years.

In addition, meeting my father was one of the greatest dreams that came true for me. It was like being a desert in need of water and given a satisfying drink. It was something that I had hoped for every single day of my life. This is not something I can find words to describe because the absence of my father hurt me so much, and I always thought that his presence would mean so much to me. Even now, as I am writing about it, tears cannot stop flowing down my cheeks. If you are reading this book and you do not have a father, I get you. If you have a father, but you do not have a relationship with him, or your parents got separated or divorced while you were still young, I get it too. It is a different setup, but the same situation. Missing my father made me feel like I was an incomplete child. When I saw other kids with their fathers, I would become jealous and I cried on the inside. I always wanted to know what it felt like to have a father and what a difference it would make in my life. I experienced living with my stepfather who was supposed to represent my father, but the thirst of having my own father was always there. Not knowing my father at all was even worse because I did not have a mental picture of him when I thought about him. I did not have a physical picture of him either, so I did not know what he looked like. Maybe if I had a picture of my father when I was growing up, I would have talked or had a conversation with him every day by thinking that he would answer me back. It seemed like I would sit on the front porch every day and expect somebody to come and introduce himself to me as my father. Even though I could not see my earthly father, I was always in contact with my Heavenly Father who never turned me down when I called on His name.

No one knows what tomorrow brings, but we all hope it is better than yesterday.

Chapter Four

GOD IS ALWAYS RIGHT BESIDE ME THROUGH THE STORMS

Whatever is going on in your life, there is always someone who is worse than you are.

The harder the storm, the greater the victory. I never knew I was going to experience so much in my life and still be standing. That is one of the reasons I am confident God Almighty is always by my side to give me strength when nobody else can.

Even when you try to explain to someone what is going on in your life, how you really feel in the inside, or what you go through on a regular basis, a human being is not going to completely understand. I recall being in a situation where my faith was being tested for a period of time in my life. That temptation I faced was against everything I believe. Another word, it was contrary with my body, soul, and spirit and everything around me, which made things more complicated and more irresistible for me to overcome with my own natural strength. I personally did not believe something like that was happening to me, but I could not fight it any longer. I prayed about the situation so God could help me come out of that mindset, but nothing happened. I prayed and fasted, but the feelings were getting stronger every day. I told a couple of friends about it in order for them to pray for me, but all they did was gossip about it. I also told my close family about it, but they simply told me to follow my heart. However, like every human being, they talked about the situation behind my back. Some of them told me to go for it while others told that it was wrong; sometimes, one person would tell me to do it and not to do it at the same time, which made me confused.

That was one of the hardest decisions for me to make in my life. I do know that there is a supernatural God who created the universe with everything in it who knows exactly what is going on in the inside of me. Sometimes, some decisions we make are foolish and we cannot take them back. All we feel like doing is to leave this planet and be transferred to another part of it, but this is not reality. The certainty is we have to face the result of our mistakes no matter what. The same way we did not ask God to create us nor did we choose to be born of our parents, nor did we choose our race, our ethnic background, or our social or economic status, the same way we cannot wish to take our lives away. I attempted to do it many times, but I remember that there are many people who depend on me--either socially, economically, or psychologically. I realize that I have to keep on moving regardless of my situation.

As long as the person has ears to hear, sometimes that is all that matters. Never let burdens, heartaches, or emotional distress draw you down. There is a solution for every problem; it may be hard to believe, but every problem has a solution and every question has an answer, even though most of them are left unanswered. It does not matter what kind of past issues that you are dealing with. It can be sexual abuse, emotional abuse, physical abuse, financial abuse, or/and all kinds of abuse. Unless you deal with it, face it, talk about, express your feelings toward it either to/with the person who caused it or somebody else, it will always haunt you, and you will become a slave to it. It is time for me and every person reading this book to be set free from abuse, no matter what kind it is. Enough is enough. No more. We were created by God to be free from all bondages. In fact, even if we were slaves after the fall of Adam and Eve, Jesus came to pay the price. After His death, the veil was torn apart, every broken heart was healed completely, every yolk was broken, and every human being who accepted the blood was set free forever. We are free indeed. The power to deal with your hurt is within you and it is up to you to decide whether or not your pain will dominate you. Through the blood of Jesus everything is possible.

Chapter Five

GOD ALLOWS STRUGGLES IN OUR LIVES TO SHAPE OUR CHARACTER

In the land of Uz there lived a man whose name was Job. This man was blameless and upright; he feared God and shunned evil. He had seven sons and three daughters, and he owned seven thousand sheep, three thousand camels, five hundred yoke of oxen and five hundred donkeys, and had a large number of servants. He was the greatest man among all the people of the East. His sons used to hold feasts in their homes on their birthdays, and they would invite their three sisters to eat and drink with them. When a period of feasting had run its course, Job would make arrangements for them to be purified. Early in the morning he would sacrifice a burnt offering for each of them, thinking, "Perhaps my children have sinned and cursed God in their hearts." This was Job's regular custom. One day the angels came to present themselves before the LORD, and Satan also came with them. The LORD said to Satan, "Where have you come from?" Satan answered the LORD, "From roaming throughout the earth, going back and forth on it." Then the LORD said to Satan, "Have you considered my servant Job? There is no one on earth like him; he is blameless and upright, a man who fears God and shuns evil." "Does Job fear God for nothing?" Satan replied. "Have you not put a hedge around him and his household and everything he has? You have blessed the work of his hands, so that his flocks and herds are spread throughout the land. But now stretch out your hand and strike everything he has, and he will surely curse you to your face." The LORD said to Satan, "Very well, then, everything he has is in your power, but on the man himself do not lay a finger." Then Satan went out from the presence of the LORD. One day when Job's sons and daughters were feasting and drinking wine at the oldest brother's house, a messenger came to Job and said, "The oxen were plowing and the donkeys were grazing nearby, and the Sabeans attacked and made off with them. They put the servants to the sword, and I am the only one who has escaped to tell you!" While he was still speaking, another messenger came and said, "The fire of God fell from the heavens and burned up the sheep and the servants, and I am the only one who has escaped to tell you!" While he was still speaking, another messenger came and said, "The Chaldeans formed three raiding parties and swept down on your camels and made off with them. They put the servants to the sword, and I am the only one who has escaped to tell you!" While he was still speaking, yet another messenger came and said, "Your sons and daughters were feasting and drinking wine at the oldest brother's house, when suddenly a mighty wind swept in from the desert and struck the four corners of the house. It collapsed on them and they are dead, and I am the only one who has escaped to tell you!" At this, Job got up and tore his robe and shaved his head. Then he fell to the ground in worship and said: "Naked I came from my mother's womb, and naked I will depart. The LORD gave and the LORD has taken away; may the name of the LORD be praised."In all this, Job did not sin by charging God with wrong-doing. – Job 1 (NIV)

Do not judge anyone based on an unplanned action. Never say you will never do something somebody else did, does, or is doing because one never knows what s/he would do when dealing with life circumstances. Everybody has his/her testing time in life. The Bible explained Job was a righteous man, but his faith was tested. A testing time is when one's strengths and weaknesses come face to face with reality, and at that time the person who is going through the dilemma is capable of discovering his/her true self. A testing time helps us become more dependent on God while we grow stronger in our faith. Nobody ever remains the same person s/he was before a testing period. During a testing moment is when our character is truly shaped, and it trains us to approach life with a different perspective. It also teaches us to make better decisions. For instance, when somebody thinks twice before reacting or making a decision, that person commits fewer errors and mistakes. Remember, errors are things that individuals do in life that can be fixed or corrected, while mistakes are things that people do that will never be fixed or corrected, but something is definitely learned from it. Never talk about or discuss a topic that you do not know well. If you do so, you will sound just like a noisy drum that has nothing inside. Everything that happens to a person s/he will always learn something from it, no matter how.

Keep trying until you succeed and never give up.

Haven't you ever been in a place in your life when you feel like the whole world is against you no matter what you do? You attend to all kinds of prayers, join forty-day fasts, participate in Bible studies, pay your tithes and give donations or special offerings, but nothing seems to be happening in your life. I am talking about when you try everything possible, but nothing goes up and nothing goes down. One of the reasons we go through so many difficulties is because we are not home yet (2 Corinthians 4:17). The Word of God says, "In the world we will have tribulations, but take courage, for He has overcome this world" (John 16:33). It does not matter what people go through year after year, as long as God is in control, there is nothing to worry about. God was in control of Job's life when Job lost all his possessions, and had to bury all of his children. Job realized he came to earth naked and naked had return back to the ground. Job was also reminded everything he had belonged to God, so if what he had was taken away from him, God's name should still be glorified. Therefore, our current status should never determine the level of our worship to God. We need to learn to worship no matter what our circumstance may be. Just take a deep breath and relax. If God is with us, who can be against us? No visible or invisible creations can separate us from God's love. He is faithful, and His mercy endures forevermore. Amen.

Chapter Six

THE TRUE PEACE IS FOUND IN THE PRESENCE OF THE ALMIGHTY

"The true peace is found in the presence of the almighty." - John 20:19

What is going on in a person's mind daily is mysterious; therefore, if we cannot say anything good about a situation, do not say anything at all.

It is hard to be still when the world around you is moving at a high speed. It is not easy to remain calm in the middle of a storm. It can be extremely difficult to be quiet when everything around you is loud.

There were times I thought I was going to lose my mind, but God was there with me every step of the way. There were times that I thought God was not hearing me or maybe I was not hearing Him. I cannot take it anymore. Sometimes I felt like yelling at the top of my lungs. I tried to talk to as many people as possible about it in order to see if I could be delivered from my feelings, but of course, everybody goes through their own life circumstances. Nobody on this planet can help you except for God. However, God feels distant when we need Him. It is hard to be still when your life is falling apart. As long as I know that, I am right with God; but how do I know that? Am I comparing myself with the people around me who do whatever they feel like doing and at the same time they sound and look like everything is going well for them? Did God speak to me and I did not hear Him or what? Or I am too busy focusing on my problems, or is it because I want things to go my way in my time? Is this some type of test? I also remember God will never give us something that we cannot handle. This means if I am going through it, it is most likely because I am able to handle it. Most importantly, nothing we go through is a surprise to God.

Jesus Calms the Storm

Then he got into the boat and his disciples followed him. Suddenly a furious storm came up on the lake, so that the waves swept over the boat. But Jesus was sleeping. The disciples went and woke him, saying, "Lord, save us! We're going to drown!" He replied, "You of little faith, why are you so afraid?" Then he got up and rebuked the winds and the waves, and it was completely calm. The men were amazed and asked, "What kind of man is this? Even the winds and the waves obey him!"-Matthew 8:23-27 (NIV)

When Jesus was on the boat with His disciples, He was sleeping in the middle of the storm (Matthew 8:24, NIV). What king of storm you are facing at this season in your life? Did you lose a loved one, a child, a pet, a spouse, a parent, a family member, or a best friend? Or maybe you are going through a divorce, an unplanned pregnancy, you lost your job and are unable to find another one? What is really going on with you right now? Can you even identify your dilemma, which represents your storm? Keep in mind this situation may be a set up to take you to the next level in your journey. The Bible said when the storm started the disciples were afraid and panicking. They did not know what to do because the storm was increasingly getting stronger every moment. Can you relate to those disciples? Do you know what to do in your situation? Who can you call? Haven't you already tried everything? Now what? The good news is the Peacemaker was on the boat. When Jesus finally woke up, He simply rebuked the winds and the waves and the storm stopped immediately.

You have been in this situation long enough! It is time to transition to a new dimension. Jesus is getting ready to rebuke your problems if you allow Him. Alleluia! All you need is a few words from the Master. *Peace! Be! Still!* Let us call every problem in the atmosphere right at this moment to be still because Jesus is in control of the visible and the invisible. Turn all your worries over to Jesus. He can make the impossible become possible. All you need to do is to believe. Jesus is the answer to your questions and the solution to your problems. After you have done all you can, now is the time give it all to the peacemaker whose name is Jesus. His name is above every name. Go ahead--trade all your sorrow, worries, discomforts, and sickness with the *peace* of the Lord!

Ending prayer

Dear Heavenly Father, in the name of Jesus of Nazareth, I pray over this reader to whom blessings should flow abundantly in every angle of his/her life. I pray every chain, strong hole, hurt, misunderstanding, and generational curse render powerless from this day and forever more. Lord, I pray that the power of Holy Spirit will fill the emptiness in this reader's life. I pronounce the blessings of Abraham upon this reader's mind, soul, spirit, and body. Lord, I thank you for his/her life. Thank you for everything that You brought him/her through. Thank you for keeping him/her alive up to this day, Lord. Thank you that he/she will live, so he/she can testify the glory of the living God. Alleluia. I Pray in Jesus' name, Amen.

If you agree and believe this prayer will come to pass in your life from generation to generation, simply lift up your hand and begin to praise the Lord like you have never done before. Praise Him, dance before Him, glorify His holy name. Shout "Alleluia" from the deepest part of your being! Say yes, Lord. Thank you, Jesus.

If you have not accepted Christ as your Lord and Savior, please ask Him to come to your life by praying the following prayer:

"Father, I know that I have broken your laws and my sins have separated me from you. I am truly sorry, and now I want to turn away from my past sinful life toward you. Please forgive me, and help me avoid sinning again. I believe that your son, Jesus Christ died for my sins, was resurrected from the dead, is alive, and hears my prayer. I invite Jesus to become the Lord of my life, to rule and reign in my heart from this day forward. Please send your Holy Spirit to help me obey You, and to do Your will for the rest of my life. In Jesus' name I pray, Amen." (Ref. http://www.allaboutgod.com/prayer-of-salvation.htm#sthash.sy5F4FvN.dpuf)

PEACE! BE STILL!

Psalm 29:11: The LORD gives strength to his people; the LORD blesses his people with peace

Psalm 119:165: Great peace has they who love your law, and nothing can make them stumble.

Isaiah 26:3: You will keep in perfect peace him whose mind is steadfast, because he trusts in you.

John 14:27: Peace I leave with you, My peace I give to you; not as the world gives do I give to you. Let not your heart be troubled, neither let it be afraid.

March 1, 2011 **Written by Marie Nadeige Maurice**
To God be all the glory and honor forever and ever!

Jehovah Shalom
Bring peace to our mind
Peace to our heart every day (twice)
Jehovah Shalom
Bring peace to our soul
Peace to our life everyday (twice)

Peace to our mind, to our hear to our soul
Peace to our life everyday (twice both lines)

Jehovah Shalom
Bring peace to our home
Peace to our church every day (twice)
Jehovah Shalom
Bring peace to the world
Peace all over the world (twice)

Peace to our home, to the church, to the world
Peace all over the world (twice both lines)

CPSIA information can be obtained
at www.ICGtesting.com
Printed in the USA
LVOW01s0258230216

476271LV00007B/74/P